BETTER WAY BOOKS

D0626863

FIRMING
YOUR
FIGURE

Cover design: Jeff Hapner
Illustrations: Lenn Martinez

ISBN 0-88176-305-5

Printed in Canada

CONTENTS

FIRMING UP FOR A BETTER FIGURE

This exercise program is designed to give you a taut, lean figure and renewed energy. The program incorporates basic principles of weight training—the fastest and most efficient method of toning muscles, increasing strength, and shaping areas that help your figure look its best.

Of course, firming the muscles is not enough for a well-proportioned appearance. Total re-shaping and conditioning demand an adequate mixture of exercise to improve strength, flexibility, and endurance.

This program is not "weight lifting," a competitive sport testing power and strength. Nor is it a conventional "body-building" program designed to sculpt the muscles into hard, defined, large symmetrical masses. We use the principles of weight (or "resistance") training to accelerate your conditioning efforts and to give you results that last. Please note, however, consult your doctor before beginning this or any other program of physical exercise.

You will probably find your greatest gains will be made early in the program. As you continue, a plateau will eventually be reached, and increased resistance and repetition of exercises will be necessary if you are to make progress. Keep working—when you stop, you lose firmness and strength within 7 to 10 days.

A number of other changes may accompany your strength gains: increased muscle size, increased lean muscle mass, and decreased fat in the muscle. Weight training will also improve quickness and endurance.

Endurance is the muscle's ability to contract continuously without tiring. Doing 10 repetitions of an exercise may be exhausting when you first begin, but as your endurance improves, you may be able to do 3 sets of 10 repetitions without feeling taxed.

Soreness in the muscles following exercise is normal, especially if you have not worked this vigorously for a while or have never worked with weights before. An overall soreness usually occurs 4 to 8 hours after exercise. This disappears and a more localized soreness results 8 to 24 hours later (the second-day syndrome). As the muscle accommodates its increased load, soreness disappears until you advance to the next level of resistance or intensity.

Emotions and muscles go hand in hand. Be determined to succeed on this program and concentrate all your efforts toward attaining your goals. Your mental attitude is as important as the program itself. A lean, taut figure glowing with health and energy can be yours, if you want it badly enough. Don't regard this as just another exercise program. It's not. This one can revitalize you.

FIGURE–FIRMING PROGRAM

Each day of this program is designed with a specific purpose. Weight training should be done every other day to attain maximum results. The first day offers a series of general conditioning, flexibility, endurance, and muscle toning exercises. The following day involves weight training. This pattern will be followed throughout the week with three days of overall conditioning exercises and three days of weight training. The seventh day is more demanding than the preceding days and combines conditioning and weight training exercises. Do not skip a day of the overall conditioning exercises. These are an integral part of a balanced body-shaping program.

Warming Up. Each day of the program consists of a warm up. The warm up increases body temperature and prepares muscles for action. For each degree body temperature rises, a parallel rise in the metabolic rate and release of oxygen to the body also takes place. The nerve impulses are heightened, and a state of readiness is achieved. An adequate warm up routine also reduces the possibility of injury.

The warm up should be vigorous enough to raise the body temperature and cause you to "break a sweat," but it should not be carried to the point of fatigue. It should consist of exercises that involve several muscle groups and should raise the pulse rate considerably.

During the warm up, the breathing rate should increase sharply in the beginning and gradually level off as the heart and lungs adapt to the body's pace. The normal breathing rate is between 10 and 25 breaths per minute, though the rate will depend on the individual body and its degree of conditioning. This rate is elevated considerably during exercise. In fact, the breathing rate actually goes up just *before* exercise begins, as a "get set" reaction from the brain.

If you feel a little bit hot and breathless from the warm up, you know it has accomplished its purpose, and you should be ready to proceed with the remaining exercises.

The general conditioning exercises should be done at varying tempos. You may prefer to perform some exercises to lively paced music and even increase the tempo of the music as you progress. Many of the warm up exercises can be done at a fast tempo, and will thus improve your power and speed. They will also help you burn off more calories.

Stretching. Stretching should be done every day to keep the muscles, joint, and connective tissue pliable. Most of the stretches in this program are the slow or gradual type. They lengthen the muscles while minimizing chances of tearing muscle fibers or connective tissue. Proceed with the stretch slowly until the muscles and ligaments have stretched far enough for you to feel "stretch pain" or discomfort. Hold the position for five seconds, allowing for full extension, then relax by releasing the stretch slowly. As your flexibility improves, you may want to hold the stretch longer to get greater extension. But never "overstretch." Your muscles and ligaments will give you signs of when you are stretching too far. Pay attention to these signs!

Resistance Training. The weight training exercises are called "isotonic" movements. Isotonic refers to the moving of a body segment or some resistive force (a weight) by shortening or lengthening the muscle. In an isotonic contraction the greatest strength gain is earned during the beginning of the movement as you overcome inertia. The movement should generally begin with the muscles in the "on stretch" or lengthened position, and then move to the contracted position. Do the weight exercises very slowly. Concentrate on the muscles being used. Speed is not important in this part of the program. Make sure you carry the exercise through its full range of motion and follow up with the stretching movement prescribed for that muscle/joint area.

Notice that a great many of the exercises are done with a straight arm. If this makes the exercise difficult in the beginning, or if excessive strain on the elbow is felt, bend the arm slightly.

The weight training program is designed to work opposing sets of muscles alternately. So follow the format and do not skip or choose the exercise you like or the ones you feel are best for you. If you miss a day or two of the program, go back to the first general conditioning day when you begin again.

Cool Down. Each workout should be ended with a cool down. It is a helpful and fitting end to an exercise routine. The cool down helps return the circulation and breathing to normal, and mentally and physically eases you back into the day's activities.

CHOOSING THE RIGHT WEIGHT

If you have never done any weight training, select a weight with which you feel comfortable for ten repetitions of an exercise. At first the weight should be light, perhaps 1 or 1½ pounds. It is better to begin light than to risk injury by using a weight that is *too* heavy. Be sure the exercises are done exactly as indicated. As you advance, follow the "Progressive Resistance Schedule."

PROGRESSIVE RESISTANCE SCHEDULE

2-Week Period	Weight (in pounds)	Sets Per Exercise	Repetitions
1st	1	1	10
2nd	1½	1	10
3rd	1½	2	10
4th	1½	3	10
5th	3	1	10
6th	3	2	10
7th	3	3	10
8th	5	1	5-7
9th	5	2	5-7
10th	5	3	5-7

Should you choose to add more weight, do fewer repetitions at first. Do not try to add too much weight too quickly. *For the exercises we have selected,* we recommend that you use no more than five-pound weights. If you have advanced to this weight but still find it is not comfortable, work with the three-pound weight for a while longer. If you have done previous weight training, start with an intermediate weight (1½ to 3 pounds) and proceed at your own rate.

The prescribed number of repetitions for a given exercise is called a "set." Thus, if the Progressive Resistance Schedule calls for two sets of an exercise in which ten repetitions are suggested, do the ten repetitions of the movement, rest briefly, then repeat the movement ten more times. The amount of rest between sets will vary with your conditioning. Take no more than a minute unless you are experiencing pain or severe discomfort.

Check your figure development by taking measurements of your bust, waist, hips, thighs, arms, etc. at the beginning of the program and every two weeks thereafter. You should be able to see progress in a short time. If you feel you are overdeveloping a group of muscles, drop down to a lower weight and substitute a general conditioning day for one of the weight training days. Also emphasize flexibility movements.

BREATHING

The body's breathing mechanism is really efficient and, under most conditions, will respond automatically to increased demands during exercise. As you perform the general conditioning exercises, keep the mouth open and breathe normally.

You will become slightly short of breath as you exercise, but, if you continue work, you may catch a "second wind," which occurs when the lungs adapt to their extra work load and breathing becomes more comfortable. Don't be afraid to push yourself a little bit. Some huffing and puffing is necessary to increase your level of fitness.

While we do not emphasize any particular breathing pattern in the general conditioning exercises, we do suggest that you observe a few guidelines on breathing while you are weight training.

Never hold the breath or force-breathe during an exercise. This may cause excessive pressure on the blood vessels and lead to dizziness or even fainting. Instead, try to control your breathing. Controlled breathing stabilizes the body and permits it to operate under the increased demands of weight training. You should develop a breathing rhythm during your exercises. Inhale as you prepare to lift the weight, and exhale as you lift. You will develop a pattern of breathing that will feed the muscles with oxygen and rid the body of the carbon dioxide it is producing. Again, breathe in as you relax, breathe out as you lift.

Do not purposely hyperventilate by taking

deep breaths before exercising. This can upset the oxygen/carbon-dioxide balance in the body and thus cause dizziness.

SOME HELPFUL TIPS
To achieve your figure and fitness goals, movements must be repeated. This applies to general fitness exercises as well as to the weight training program exercises. The number of repetitions indicated in each exercise is a goal. If you cannot achieve this goal at the beginning without experiencing fatigue, do half the number indicated and gradually work up to the prescribed number of repetitions. If the number of repetitions can be done with ease, you may either increase the number of repetitions or sets as indicated in the "Progressive Resistance Schedule" or add more weight for that particular exercise.

"As far as possible" is the phrase frequently used in suggesting the range of movement for a given exercise. Since everyone's structure is different and there are joint and muscle limitations, this means as far as *you* can move the body or limb. Never force a movement to the point where it becomes extremely painful.

There is no right time of day for every individual to exercise. The best time is when you feel like exercising—when you have the time and energy. It may be morning, noon, or night. Any time is fine, as long as you do it!

DAY ONE

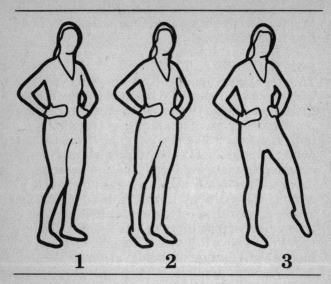

1   2   3

WARM UP #1

1. Stand, feet slightly apart, knees slightly bent, hands on hips. This exercise will increase the circulation in the legs.

2. Lift onto the toes, then lower to the heels. Repeat this up-and-down movement 25 times. Increase count as your strength improves.

3. Rest 5 counts. Shake one leg, then the other. You should feel a tingling in the legs.

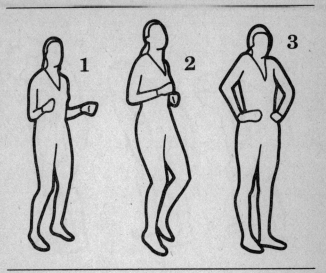

WARM UP # 2

1. Stand, feet slightly apart, arms held at waist height.

2. Lift knees in an easy run in place. Keep the mouth open and breathe normally. (Start with 50 steps on each foot and work up to 200.)

3. Rest 5 counts. Place hands on hips and lift the shoulders. You should be slightly out of breath.

NECK/SHOULDERS EXERCISE

1. Stand, with feet wide apart, knees bent, hands on knees, torso inclined forward, back flat, head down. This will strengthen the muscles in the back of the neck and help relieve tension in this area.

2. Press hands into knees to support the back, and raise the head up and forward so that you are looking straight ahead. (Do not look at ceiling. This will cause too much pressure on the cervical nerve.) Press the chin forward. Repeat 5 times. Work up to 10.

3. Lower head, bend the knees, round the back, lift shoulders and slowly come to a standing position.

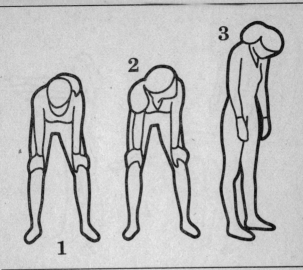

NECK/SHOULDERS EXERCISE

1. Stand with knees bent, feet wide apart, hands on knees, torso inclined forward, back flat, head down. This will strengthen the muscles at the sides of the neck.

2. Press hands into knees to support the back, and turn the head very slowly to the left, back to the center, then to the right. Do not jerk the head. Repeat 10 times.

3. Bend knees, lift shoulders, round the back, come to a standing position. Drop head and press the chin to the chest. Hold, then lift head. Repeat 5 times.

DAY ONE

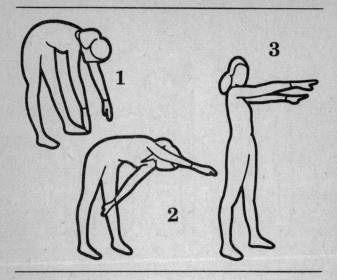

ARMS EXERCISE

1. Stand, feet wide apart, torso inclined forward, head down, arms hanging loosely. You will feel this in the shoulders and upper back.

2. Swing the arms forward and back, alternating right and left, 20 times. Make sure the swing is as high as the head.

3. Place hands on knees, round the back, and come to a standing position. Extend arms forward. Stretch right arm as far as possible, then the left. Relax. Repeat 10 times.

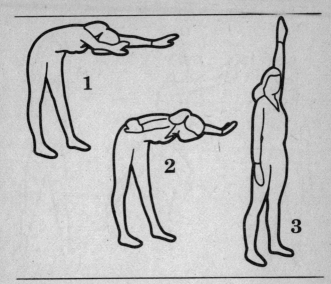

ARMS EXERCISE

1. Stand, feet wide apart, torso inclined forward, head down, arms extended straight forward. You should feel this in the upper arms and shoulders.

2. Turn palms outward, and pull arms to sides and back; bend elbows, and extend arms forward again as in a swimming breast stroke. Repeat 20 times.

3. Place hands on knees, round the back, and come to a standing position. Extend the left arm overhead and stretch as high as possible. Lower arm. Repeat 10 times with each arm.

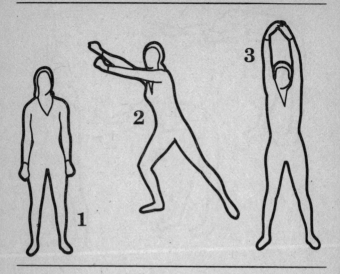

UPPER TORSO/BUST EXERCISE

1. Stand, feet apart, arms hanging loosely at sides, hands in a fist, knees slightly bent.

2. Lunge to right: right knee bent, left leg extended. At same time, swing both arms to right, stopping at shoulder height. Swing back to starting position. Repeat 10 times to each side.

3. Clasp the hands and stretch the arms directly overhead. Hold. Relax. Repeat 5 times.

UPPER TORSO/BUST EXERCISE

1. Stand feet wide apart, torso bent forward, head down, arms hanging loosely toward the floor, hands in a fist, knees bent slightly.

2. Keeping the right leg straight, bend the left knee and swing both arms to the left and upward to head height. Swing back to starting position. Repeat 10 times to each side.

3. Stand, clasp the hands, and turn palms up toward the ceiling. Stretch and hold. Relax. Repeat 5 times.

LATERALS/WAIST EXERCISE

1. Stand, feet wide apart, knees slightly bent, arms in an arc overhead, right hand clasping left. This one is fantastic for the waistline.

2. Keeping the hips and knees fluid, move the arms to the left, at the same time pressing the hips to the left. Then move arms to the right, hips to the right in a rocking motion. Repeat 30 times.

3. Stand with feet apart, torso bent forward, hands clasped, arms in an arc and hanging loosely. Lift arms to head height. Lower. Repeat 5 times.

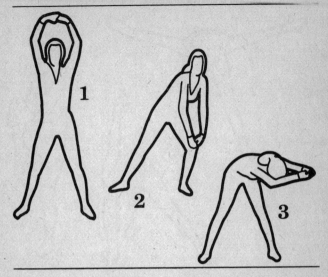

LATERALS/WAIST EXERCISE

1. Stand, feet wide apart, knees slightly bent, arms in an arc overhead, right hand clasping left.

2. Keeping the knees fluid, bend the left knee at the same time swinging the arms from overhead, touching the left knee. Return to the starting position. Repeat to the right. Continue for 15 repetitions.

3. Stand with feet apart, torso bent forward, hands clasped, arms in an arc and hanging loosely. Swing the arms to the left, stretching the trunk. Return. Repeat to the right. Continue for 10 repetitions.

HIPS/THIGHS/BUTT EXERCISE

1. Stand, feet wide apart, torso bent forward and parallel to the floor, knees slightly bent, head down.

2. Bend the left knee and touch the floor behind the left foot with the right hand. Swing the left arm up at the same time. Alternate from left to right for 10 counts.

3. Stand on right leg; slowly pull the left knee up to the chest. Hold. Release knee and lower leg to the floor. Repeat 5 times with each leg.

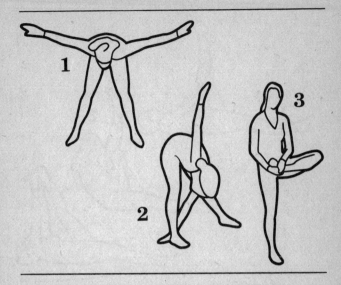

HIPS/THIGHS/BUTT EXERCISE

1. Stand, feet wide apart, torso bent forward and parallel to the floor, knees slightly bent, head down. This one is more difficult than the first exercise.

2. Bend the right knee and place the left palm on the floor behind the right heel. Swing the right arm up at the same time. Alternate from right to left for 10 counts.

3. Place hands on knees, round the back and come up slowly. Stand on right leg. Grasp the left foot with both hands; slowly pull the foot as high as possible. Lower. Repeat with right foot.

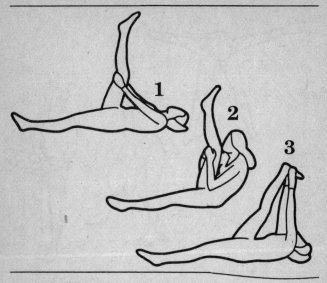

ABDOMINAL EXERCISE

1. Lie on back, right leg extended straight up, left leg forward on floor, both hands clasped behind the right leg.

2. Pull the head and shoulders up toward the leg until the chin meets the knee. Lower head and torso to floor. Repeat 5 times with each leg.

3. Grasp the bottom of the right foot with both hands. Slowly extend the right leg as straight as possible. Hold. Relax. Repeat with the left leg.

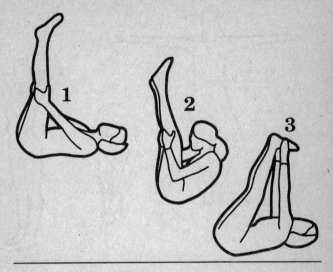

ABDOMINAL EXERCISE

1. Lie on back, both legs extended up, hands grasping both knees.

2. Pull the head and shoulders up toward the legs until the chin meets the knees. Hold. Lower head and torso to the floor. Repeat 10 times.

3. Grasp the bottoms of both feet with both hands and try to extend both legs to a straight position. Hold. Relax. Repeat 5 times.

DAY ONE

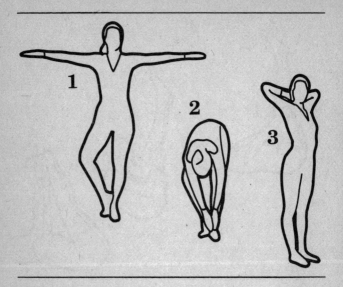

COOL DOWN # 1

1. Stand on the left leg, right leg bent, right foot against the left ankle, arms extended to the side. This is a complete relaxation stretch. Do it often.

2. Very slowly extend the arms overhead, then reach down toward the ankles. Stretch and hold for 10 counts.

3. Come up slowly to a standing position. Clasp the hands behind the neck. Press the elbows back. Relax. Repeat 5 times.

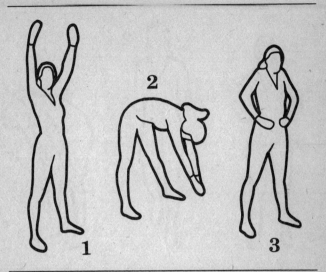

COOL DOWN # 2

1. Stand, feet wide apart, arms overhead, body relaxed. Release all your tension.

2. Bending at the waist, swing the arms toward the floor and back between the legs. Swing back to starting position. Repeat 5 times.

3. Place hands on hips. Take a deep breath while lifting the shoulders. Hold. Slowly exhale and lower the shoulders.

Day Two

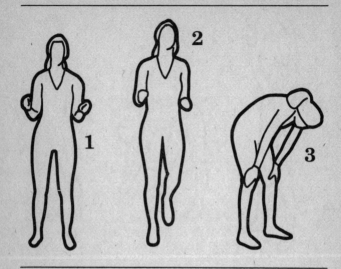

WARM UP # 1

1. Stand, feet slightly apart, knees slightly bent, arms bent at waist height.

2. Lift knees in an easy run in place for 300 counts. Keep the mouth open and breathe normally.

3. Rest for 5 counts. Place the hands on the knees, round the back, and lift the shoulders. You should be slightly out of breath but full of energy.

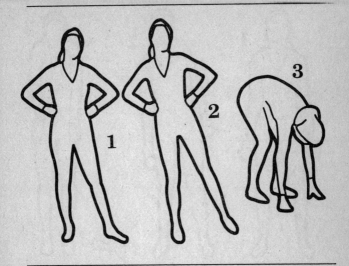

WARM UP # 2

1. Stand with weight on right leg, left leg extended to the side, hands on hips.

2. Hop up and down on the right foot 20 times. Repeat on the left foot 20 times. Alternate 20 counts on each leg for a total of 80 counts.

3. Stand, feet slightly apart, knees bent, fingertips on the floor in front of toes, head down. Keeping fingertips on the floor, slowly straighten the legs. Bend knees to starting position. Repeat 3 times.

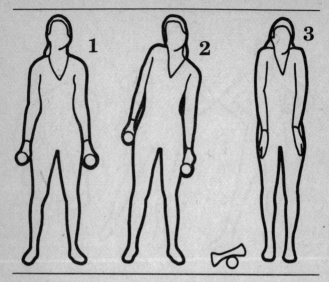

NECK/SHOULDERS EXERCISE

1. Stand, feet apart, knees slightly bent. Hold a training weight in each hand.

2. Lift the right shoulder as high as possible. Hold for 2 counts, lower to starting position. Repeat with the left shoulder. Alternate for 5 repetitions with each shoulder.

3. Place the weights down. Stand, with arms at sides. Roll the shoulders forward. Hold. Then press the shoulders back. Repeat 3 times. Your muscles should feel loose.

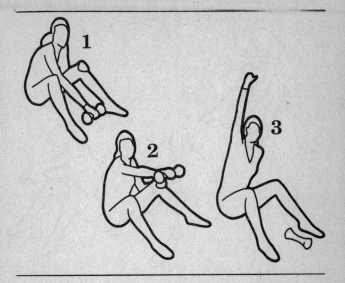

NECK/SHOULDERS EXERCISE

1. Sit on the floor, feet apart, knees bent, head relaxed. Hold the training weight palm down in the right hand, the right arm extended forward, weight on the floor.

2. Slowly lift the training weight to shoulder height. Lower to floor. Repeat 10 times with each arm.

3. Place the weight down. Extend the right arm straight up as high as possible, turning the palm back and toward the ceiling. Stretch. Hold. Lower arm. Repeat with the left arm.

DAY TWO

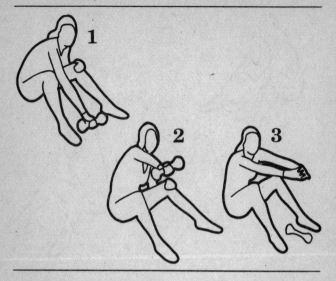

ARMS EXERCISE

1. Sit on the floor, feet apart, knees bent, head relaxed. Hold the training weight in the right hand, extend the right arm forward, weight on the floor.

2. Twist the right arm so that the palm and weight are turned up toward the ceiling. Slowly lift the weight to shoulder height. Lower to floor. Repeat 10 times with each arm.

3. Place the weight down. Shake both arms to relax muscles. Clasp the hands and turn the palms out. Straighten the arms and stretch them forward. Hold. Relax and bend the elbows. Repeat 5 times.

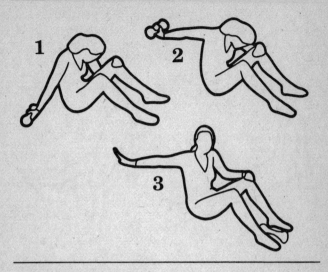

ARMS EXERCISE

1. Sit on the floor, feet apart, knees bent, head down. Hold the training weight on the floor in back of the right hip, palm and weight turned up toward the ceiling.

2. Slowly lift the weight up in back as high as possible. Hold. Lower to the floor. Repeat 10 times with each arm.

3. Place the weight down. Shake both arms to relax muscles. Raise the right arm directly out to the side at shoulder height. Reach as far as possible. Hold. Relax. Repeat 5 times with each arm.

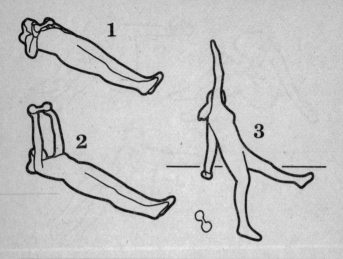

UPPER TORSO/BUST EXERCISE

1. Lie on back, legs extended forward, head on the floor, elbows on the floor at sides, both hands holding the training weight across the chest.

2. Extend the training weight upward at arm's length directly over the chest. Return to starting position. Repeat 10 times.

3. Sit, legs wide apart, left hand on floor at left side. With body weight on the left hand and the heels, raise hips off floor; swing the right arm and torso to the left. Swing arm back and switch body weight to right hand. Repeat to the right. Alternate each arm 10 times.

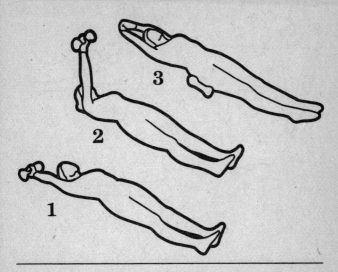

UPPER TORSO/BUST EXERCISE

1. Lie flat on back, left arm at side. Hold the training weight in the right hand, palm up, right arm straight along the floor behind the head.

2. With a straight right arm, raise the weight to a 90-degree position directly overhead. Hold. Return weight to the starting position. Repeat 10 times with each arm.

3. Place the weight down. Clasp the hands and press them back behind the head along the floor. Stretch and hold. Relax. Repeat 3 times.

DAY TWO

LATERALS/WAIST EXERCISE

1. Sit on the floor, feet apart, knees slightly bent, head up. Hold the training weight in both hands and extend it at arms length over the right knee.

2. Lift the weight above the right knee; swing and lower it to the left knee. Lift weight, swing it back to the right, and lower it to starting position. Repeat 10 times.

3. Place the weight down. Shake both arms to relax the muscles. Raise the arms straight out to the sides and twist them so that the palms are up toward the ceiling. Hold 3 counts. Relax. Repeat 5 times.

LATERALS/WAIST EXERCISE

1. Sit on the floor, feet apart, knees slightly bent, head up. Hold the training weight in both hands at arms length on the floor outside the right knee.

2. Lift the weight straight overhead, then lower it to the floor outside the left knee. Repeat 10 times to each side.

3. Place the weight down. Clasp hands behind the back. Lean forward and lift the arms as high as possible. Hold. Relax. Repeat 3 times.

HIPS/THIGHS/BUTT EXERCISE

1. Kneel on the hands and left knee, right leg extended directly to the side, training weight on the right ankle.

2. Keeping the knee straight, lift the right leg directly up to shoulder height. Lower. Repeat 10 times with each leg.

3. Kneel on left knee, right leg extended forward with toe up, body erect. Bend from the waist toward the extended leg and touch the right toe with the hands. Hold for 5 counts. Repeat with left leg.

HIPS/THIGHS/BUTT EXERCISE

1. Kneel on the hands and left knee, right leg extended to the side and slightly back, training weight on the right ankle.

2. Keeping the knee straight, lift the right leg and swing it toward the head as far forward as possible. Return without lowering the leg to the floor. Repeat 10 times with each leg.

3. Kneel on left knee and the left hand. Grasp the bottom of the right foot with the right hand. Extend the right leg and straighten it as much as possible. Hold for 5 counts. Relax. Repeat with left leg.

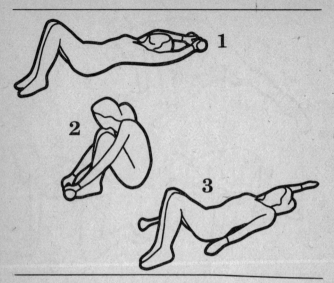

ABDOMINAL EXERCISE

1. Lie on back with knees bent, feet flat on the floor. Hold training weight in both hands, palms up, with arms extended behind the head.

2. Swing the arms forward, curl your body up into sitting position, and extend the weight beyond the knees. Touch the weight to the floor. Return to starting position. Repeat 10 times. Do not jerk the head.

3. Place the weight down. Return to starting position. Extend the right arm behind the head along the floor. Stretch as far as possible. Hold. Repeat 3 times with each arm.

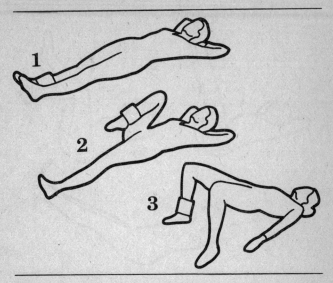

ABDOMINAL EXERCISE

1. Lie flat on your back, hands behind the head, legs extended, training weight on the right ankle. Push your back into the floor for back support.

2. Bend the right knee and bring it to the chest, extend the right leg straight up, lower leg to the floor. Repeat 10 times with each leg.

3. Place arms at the sides, bend the knees, place the feet flat on the floor and wide apart. Lift the hips up off the floor as high as possible. This will stretch the abdomen and release the pressure on the back.

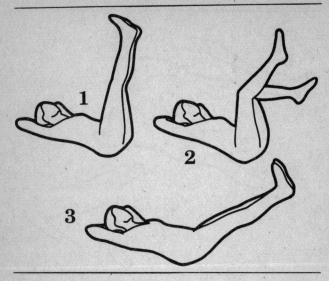

COOL DOWN # 1

1. Lie on back, hands behind the neck, legs extended straight up.

2. Kick lower legs alternately up and down for a count of 20.

3. Extend both legs up; slowly lower legs to the floor, keeping feet flat; bend knees to chest and return to starting position. Repeat 3 times.

COOL DOWN #2

1.   Lie on the floor, resting on elbows, knees bent, feet flat on the floor.

2.   Extend the legs straight up. Slowly lower both legs to the floor. Bend the knees and extend the legs up again. Repeat 5 times.

3.   Stand on the toes, feet slightly apart, hands on the floor in front of the feet. Pressing the heels back into the floor, straighten the legs. Come to a stand slowly.

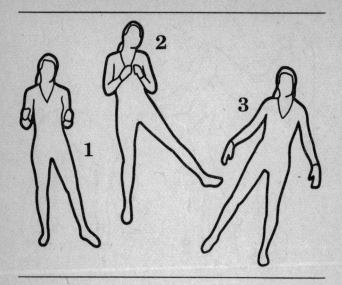

WARM UP #1

1. Stand on right leg, left leg raised off floor, arms bent at waist.

2. Hop twice on the right foot, then twice on the left foot, swinging the elbows forward and back at the same time.

3. Rest 5 counts. With the arms at the sides, shake the hands. Shake the right leg; then shake the left leg. The muscles should feel loose.

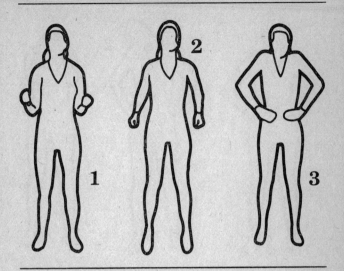

WARM UP #2

1. Stand, feet slightly apart, arms bent at waist height.

2. Jump up and down, landing lightly on the toes, for 50 counts. Increase to 200 jumps as you progress.

3. Rest 5 counts. Place hands on hips. Take a deep breath while lifting the shoulders. Hold. Slowly exhale and lower the shoulders.

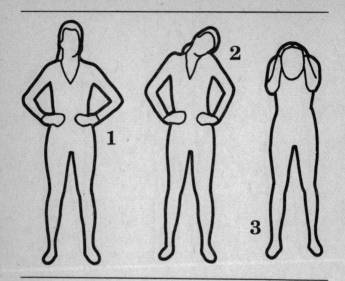

NECK/SHOULDERS EXERCISE

1. Stand, feet slightly apart, hands on hips. This is very good for tightening "jawline jowls."

2. Slowly incline the head to the left, at the same time raising the left shoulder as high as possible. (Feel the pull on the right side of the neck.) Hold for 5 counts. Relax. Repeat 2 times on each side.

3. Place the hands on the back of the head. Pull the head down until you feel the pull on the neck and shoulder muscles. Hold for 5 counts. Relax. Lift the head.

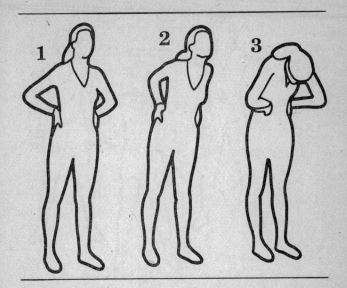

NECK/SHOULDERS EXERCISE

1. Stand, feet slightly apart, head erect, hands on hips with fingers pointed back.

2. Press the elbows and shoulders back. At the same time, move the chin forward and tilt it up. Hold for 5 counts. Relax. Repeat 3 times. (Keep the mouth closed.)

3. Lower the head. Place the chin on the chest. Pull the elbows as far forward as possible. Hold. Relax. This should release tension in the back and neck.

DAY THREE

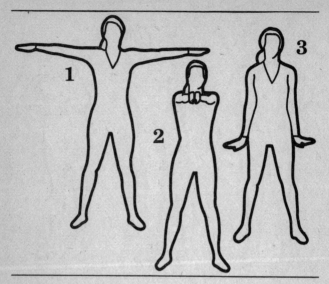

ARMS EXERCISE

1. Stand, feet wide apart, arms extended to the sides at shoulder height, palms turned down toward the floor.

2. Swing the arms forward and touch the backs of the hands together. Return to starting position. Repeat 15 times.

3. Shake arms at sides. Relax. Pull the fingers and hands back to a flat position, and straighten the arms. This will help smooth out the arm muscles.

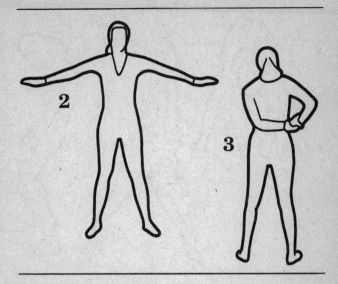

ARMS EXERCISE

1. Stand, feet wide apart, arms extended to the sides at shoulder height, palms up toward the ceiling. This will firm underarm flab.

2. Twist the arm so that the palms are up in back. Move the arms in small circles 25 times.

3. Clasp the wrists behind the back. Move the arms across the back from right to left and back again 10 times.

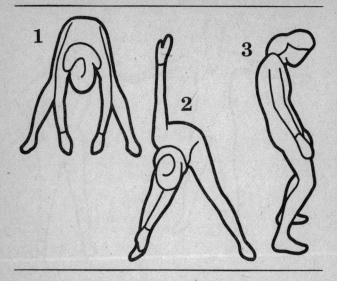

UPPER TORSO/BUST EXERCISE

1. Stand, feet wide apart, torso bent forward, head down, arms hanging loosely toward the floor, knees bent slightly. (If you have a weak back, bend only to the knees.)

2. Touch the right ankle with the left hand, at the same time raising the right arm up. Lower the right arm and swing the right hand to the left ankle, raising the left arm up. Repeat 20 times.

3. Slowly slide the hands up to the knees. Press the knees and the pelvis forward, round the back, lift the shoulders, raise the head, and come to an erect position.

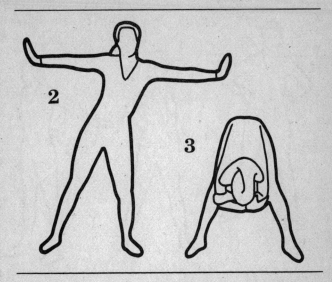

UPPER TORSO/BUST EXERCISE

1. Stand, feet wide apart, knees slightly bent, arms extended straight to the sides at shoulder height, hands pulled back from the wrist. (Imagine you are a Siamese dancer.)

2. Moving from the waist, press the torso and left arm to the left as far as possible, then move to the right in the same manner. Repeat 12 times. (Remember: nothing moves from the waist down.)

3. Clasp the elbows, lean forward, and swing the arms between the legs. Swing back up to a stretch position over the head. Hold the stretch for 5 counts.

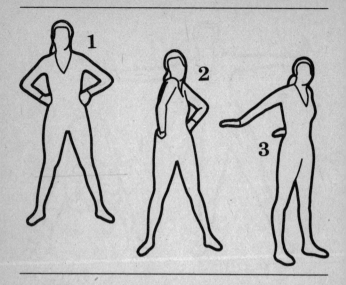

LATERALS/WAIST EXERCISE

1. Stand, feet wide apart, hands on hips, fingers turned back.

2. Roll the right shoulder forward pressing the right elbow forward and toward centerline. Return to starting position. Repeat 15 times to each side.

3. Lower arms to sides, palms facing back. Press arms straight back and up as high as possible. Lower arms. Repeat 5 times.

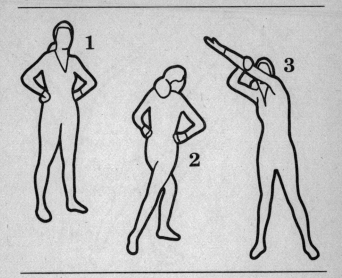

LATERALS/WAIST EXERCISE

1. Stand, feet wide apart, hands on the hips, fingers pointing back.

2. Twist the torso to the left, moving the right elbow forward and pivoting on the right toe. Swing back to starting position. Repeat 10 times to each side.

3. Extend the left arm up overhead, palm facing outward. Grasp the left elbow with the right hand, and pull the left arm across to the right as far as possible. Hold. Repeat with the right.

HIPS/THIGHS/BUTT EXERCISE

1. Stand, feet wide apart, right foot to the side, right knee bent. Lean over the right knee. Place left hand on floor next to right foot, right hand on floor at right side.

2. With the left hand on the floor, straighten the right knee and raise the right arm up. (Keep the head down and the back rounded.) Bend knee. Repeat 10 times each leg.

3. Place the hands on the knees, round the back, and slowly come to a stand. Grasp the bottom of the left foot from the inside with the left hand, and extend the leg straight out and to the side.

HIPS/THIGHS/BUTT EXERCISE

1. Stand, feet wide apart, weight on left leg, right leg extended to the side, right toe on floor, arms at sides, hands in a fist. This is a strong swinging movement.

2. Lunge to the right, bending the right knee sharply. At the same time, swing both arms to the right transferring the weight to the right leg. Return to starting position. Repeat 10 times to each side.

3. Grasp the right ankle with the right hand, lean forward, and pull the right leg back until the upper leg is at least parallel to the floor. This will stretch the thigh muscles.

DAY THREE

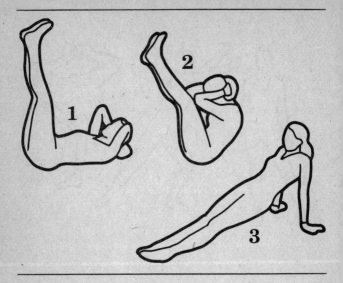

ABDOMINAL EXERCISE

1. Lie on back, legs extended straight up, hands clasped behind neck, head off the floor so that the back is rounded.

2. Sit up and touch the elbows to the knees. Lower to starting position. Repeat 5 times. Work up to 10.

3. Sit on the floor, legs extended straight forward, hands on the floor next to the hips, weight on hands and heels. Lift the body up off the floor. Stretch from the feet to the head. Press the shoulders back. Relax.

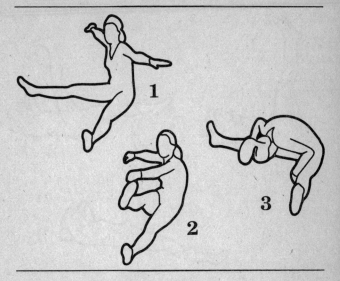

ABDOMINAL EXERCISE

1. Sit on the floor, feet wide apart, arms straight out to the sides at shoulder height.

2. Raise the right leg and swing it to the left. Touch the left hand to the right foot. Swing the leg back to starting position. Repeat 10 times with each leg. (Bring the foot to meet the hand.)

3. Return to starting position. Place hands under knees from the inside of the legs. Pull the head down toward the floor. Hold 5 counts. Relax.

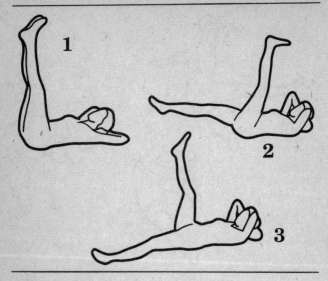

COOL DOWN #1

1. Lie on floor, legs extended straight up, hands under head.

2. Lower the right leg toward the floor and alternately swing the legs up and down, stretching toward the head. (You can rest the head on the floor or hold it up with the hands.)

3. With the legs extended up, lower the left leg to the floor. Return to the up position. Lower the right leg. Alternate 10 times with each leg.

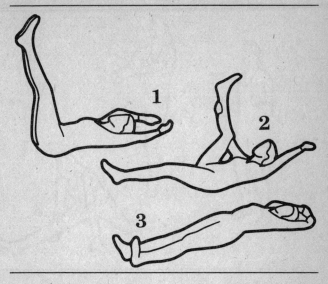

COOL DOWN #2

1. Lie on floor, legs extended straight up, arms on floor over the head.

2. As in the last exercise, alternately swing the legs up and down, stretching toward the head. At the same time, touch right hand behind right ankle, left behind left. Repeat 20 times.

3. Extend the legs forward. Clasp the hands on the floor over the head. Stretch right leg from the hip, at the same time shortening the left leg. Repeat 10 times with each leg.

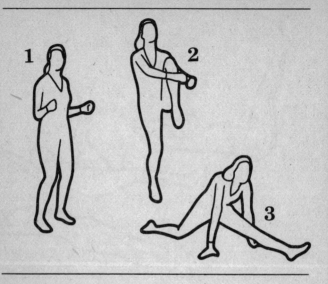

WARM UP #1

1. Stand feet slightly apart, knees bent, arms at waist height. Get ready for vigorous movement.

2. Hop continuously on the right foot. On every second count, raise the left knee up to the chest and encircle it with both arms. Lower knee. Alternate legs every 10 hops for a total of 100 counts.

3. Rest 5 counts. Lean forward and place hands on the floor. Slide left leg forward between the hands, right leg straight back. Stretch legs as far as possible. Lift up. Switch leg positions and repeat. Alternate sides 4 times.

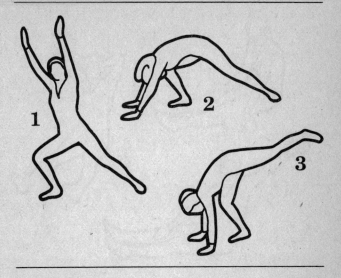

WARM UP # 2

1. Stand in lunge position, right knee bent, left leg extended straight back, right toe forward, left toe pointed to the side, arms held overhead.

2. Bend from the waist and touch the hands to the floor in front of the right foot. Return to starting position. Repeat 10 times to each side.

3. From the lunge position, lean forward and place the hands on the floor in front of the right foot. Raise the left leg straight up and down 10 times. Repeat with right leg.

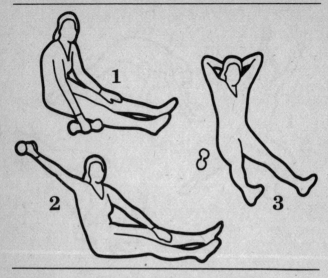

NECK/SHOULDERS EXERCISE

1. Sit on the floor, legs apart, knees bent in comfortable position. Hold the training weight palm down in the right hand beside the right knee. Place the left hand on the left knee for back support.

2. Raise the weight in an arc overhead; lower it to the floor behind the hips. Swing back to starting position. Repeat 10 times with each arm.

3. Place the weight down. Place hands on shoulders and lift the elbows as high as possible. Lower. Repeat 5 times.

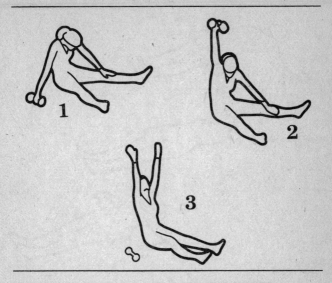

NECK/SHOULDERS EXERCISE

1. Sit on the floor, legs apart, knees bent in comfortable position, head down. Hold training weight palm down on floor in right hand, right arm directly to the side.

2. Raise the right arm to a position straight overhead, the back of the hand toward the ear. Lower. Repeat 10 times with each arm.

3. Place the weight down. Press both elbows into sides; then stretch the arms straight overhead. Relax. Repeat 5 times.

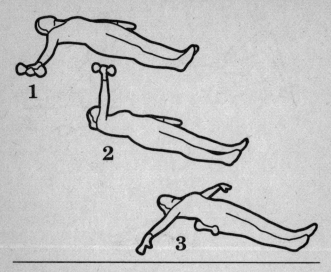

ARMS EXERCISE

1. Lie on the back, right arm extended directly to the side at shoulder level, left arm at side. Hold the training weight palm up in the right hand.

2. Raise the weight to a 90-degree position directly overhead. Lower to the floor. Repeat 10 times with each arm.

3. Place weight down. Extend both arms to sides at shoulder level. Dig the finger-tips into the floor, and try to lift the back off the floor. Hold. Lower. Repeat 5 times. (Do not raise the head.)

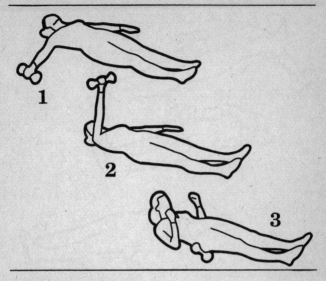

ARMS EXERCISE

1. Lie on the back, right arm extended directly to the side at shoulder level. Hold the training weight palm down in the right hand.

2. Raise the weight to a 90-degree position directly overhead. Lower to the floor. Repeat 10 times with each arm.

3. Place the weight down. With the elbows bent and the upper arms on the floor, press the arms into the floor and lift the head and shoulders up. Lower to floor. Repeat 5 times.

DAY FOUR

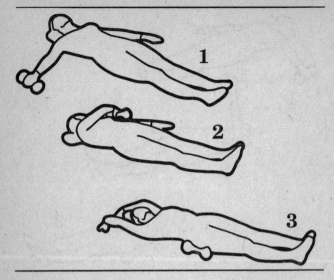

UPPER TORSO/BUST EXERCISE

1. Lie on the back, right arm extended directly to the side at shoulder level, left arm at side. Hold the training weight palm up in the right hand.

2. With the elbow bent slightly, raise the weight overhead and across the body, touching the floor on the left side. Return to starting position. Repeat 10 times with each arm.

3. Place the weight down. Reach back with both arms, and touch the floor behind the head with the fingers. Press fingertips into the floor. Hold 5 counts.

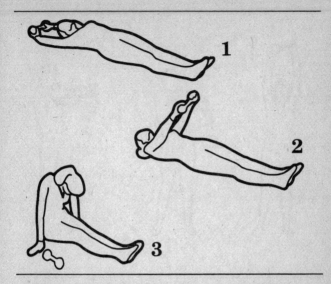

UPPER TORSO/BUST EXERCISE

1. Lie on back, legs extended straight forward, head on floor, arms extended along the floor behind the head, training weight held in both hands.

2. With the arms straight, swing the weight forward, passing overhead and touching the thighs with the weight. Swing weight back to starting position. Repeat 10 times.

3. Place the weight down. Sit on the floor, place the palms of the hands flat on the floor beside the hips. Straighten the arms and lift the hips off the floor. Bend the elbows and return to starting position. Repeat 5 times.

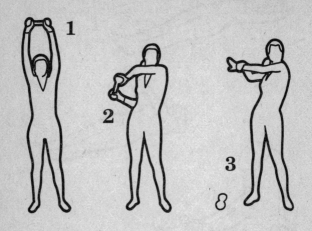

LATERALS/WAIST EXERCISE

1. Stand, feet apart. Hold training weight in both hands directly overhead.

2. Bend the elbows and lower the weight to the right side, crossing the left arm in front of the face. Return to the overhead position. Lower to the left side. Return. Repeat 10 times.

3. Place the weight down. Extend the left arm forward. Grasp the left wrist with the right hand, pull the left arm across the body to the right. Hold for 5 counts. Repeat with right arm.

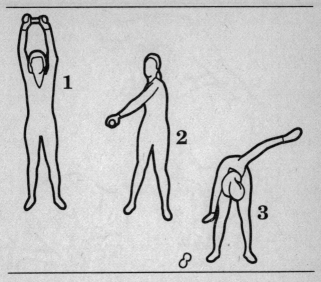

LATERALS/WAIST EXERCISE

1. Stand, feet apart. Hold training weight in both hands directly overhead.

2. Turn torso slightly to the right and lower the weight to the right hip. Swing weight back to starting position. Repeat 10 times to each side.

3. Place the weight down. Lean forward from the waist and make large circles with the arms in a long, swimming motion. Repeat 10 times.

Day Four

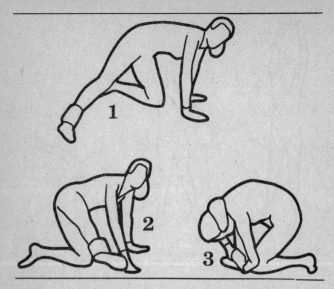

HIPS/THIGHS/BUTT EXERCISE

1. Kneel on the hands and left knee, right leg extended directly to the side, training weight on the right ankle.

2. Keeping the knee straight, lift the right leg and move it in large circles. Repeat 10 times with each leg.

3. Kneel on left knee. Place right foot in front of left knee, heel touching the knee, right toe turned to right side. Grasp right ankle with both hands and pull the torso toward the floor. Hold 5 counts. Repeat to left.

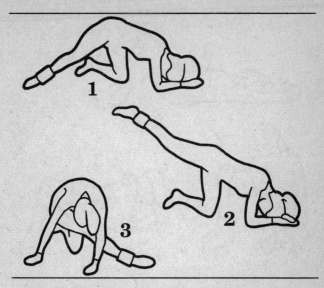

HIPS/THIGHS/BUTT EXERCISE

1. Kneel on the elbows and left knee, right leg extended straight back, training weight on the right ankle. This one will firm the buttocks.

2. Raise the right leg up and back as high as possible. Keep the knee straight. Lower leg. Repeat 10 times.

3. Kneel on left knee. Place both hands on the floor in front of the legs. Cross the right leg over the left knee and extend it to the left as far as possible. Lower the head toward the floor.

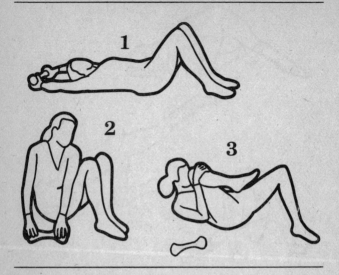

ABDOMINAL EXERCISE

1. Lie on back with knees bent, feet flat on the floor. Hold training weight in both hands, palms up, with arms extended behind the head.

2. Swing the arms forward, and curl your body up into a sitting position, at the same time twisting the torso. Touch the weight to the floor beside the right hip. Return to starting position. Repeat, twisting to left. Repeat 10 times.

3. Place the weight down. Return to starting position with knees bent, feet on the floor. Clasp right knee with both hands, lift head, and pull the knee to the nose. Hold for 5 counts. Repeat with left knee.

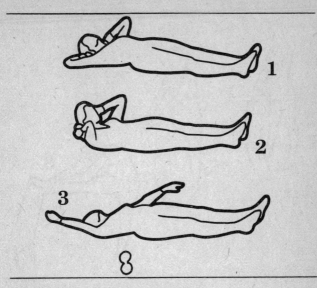

ABDOMINAL EXERCISE

1. Lie on the back, legs extended forward. Hold training weight in both hands just behind the head, elbows off the floor. (Bend the knees slightly for more back support.)

2. Slowly curl the head and shoulders forward and up, pushing the lower back into the floor. Do not sit up. Lower to the floor. Repeat 10 times.

3. Place the weight down. Stretch the arms behind the head. Swing the left arm forward, then the right, in a back and forth motion. Touch the floor behind head with each swing.

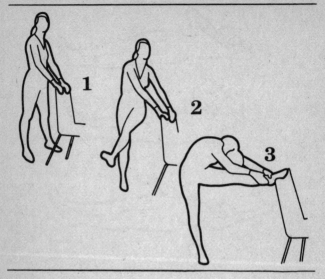

COOL DOWN #1

1. Stand, feet slightly apart, toes about 14 inches from chair, hands holding back of chair, arms straight, body erect.

2. Swing the left leg out to the left, then across the body to the right. Swing as high as possible. Return to starting position. Repeat 10 times with each leg.

3. With weight on right leg, lift left leg and place left foot on back of chair. Leg should be straight. Bend over from the waist and reach for the left ankle. Hold. Repeat with right leg.

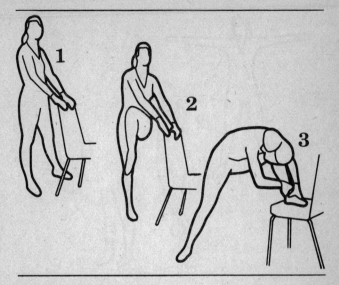

COOL DOWN #2

1. Stand, feet slightly apart, toes about 14 inches from chair, hands holding back of chair, arms straight, body erect.

2. Lift left knee to waist height, turn it toward the right, lower the left foot to the floor. Lift knee again, turn it to left side, and return to starting position. Repeat 10 times with each leg.

3. Place the left foot on the seat of the chair, bend the left knee and slowly reach for the left ankle. Hold. Repeat with the right leg.

DAY FIVE

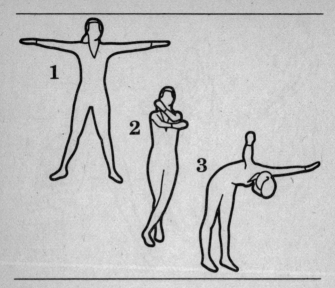

WARM UP #1

1. Stand, feet wide apart, arms extended directly to the sides at shoulder height.

2. Jump, crossing left foot in front of right foot and left arm (forward) over right. Jump again, returning to starting position. Repeat, crossing right foot in front of left and right arm over left. Continue for 20 counts.

3. Rest 5 counts. Lean forward from the waist, arms hanging loosely, head down. Move both arms in large forward circles. Do 10 repetitions.

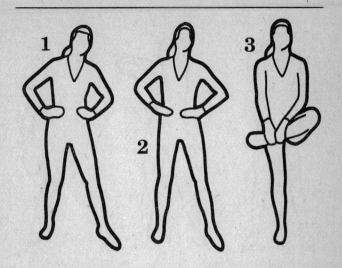

WARM UP #2

1. Stand on right leg, hands on hips, left leg raised off the floor.

2. Hop on right foot, moving in a large circle on that foot for 3 revolutions. Change to the left foot and repeat.

3. Stand on right leg. Grasp the left ankle with both hands and pull the foot to the waist. Circle the left foot 10 times. Repeat with the right foot.

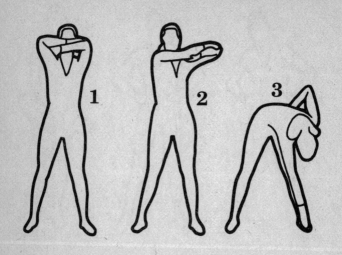

NECK/SHOULDERS EXERCISE

1. Stand, feet wide apart, arms folded in front of the eyes, hands clasping the elbows.

2. Move the arms strongly across the face to the left as far as possible. Repeat to the right. Alternate to each side for 20 repetitions.

3. Lean forward from the waist, hands on hips, head down. Touch the right hand to the left foot. Return to starting position. Touch left hand to right foot. Return. Alternate to each side 10 times.

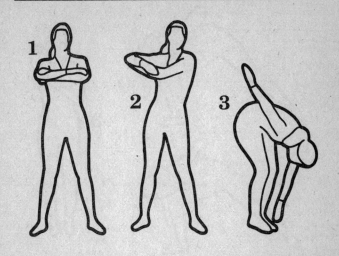

NECK/SHOULDERS EXERCISE

1. Stand, feet wide apart, arms folded in front of chest, hands clasping elbows.

2. Move the arms strongly to the right across the chest. Repeat to the left. Alternate to each side for 20 repetitions.

3. Stand, feet together, knees bent, arms at sides, torso bent forward, palms turned outward. Swing right arm back as far as possible. Return to starting position. Repeat left. Alternate to each side 10 times.

DAY FIVE

ARMS EXERCISE

1. Stand, feet wide apart, left foot turned out, right foot ahead. Lean over the bent left knee and grasp left ankle with left hand. Place right hand behind back, palm up.

2. Bending at the elbow, extend the right forearm to the straight position. Return to starting position. Repeat 10 times with each arm.

3. Stand. Place left arm behind back, palm out, and reach up the back. Reach right hand over the right shoulder, and touch the fingers of the left hand. Hold. Repeat with right arm behind back.

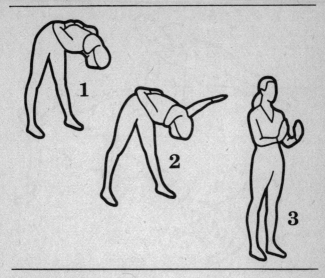

ARMS EXERCISE

1. Stand, feet wide apart, torso bent forward at the waist, head down. Place both arms behind the back, elbows bent, hands touching.

2. Extend the left arm directly to the side at shoulder level. Return to starting position. Repeat with the right arm. Alternate each arm for 10 repetitions.

3. Stand, arms at waist height, hands open, palms down. Snap the hands up from the wrist. Hold. Lower hands. Repeat 5 times.

DAY FIVE

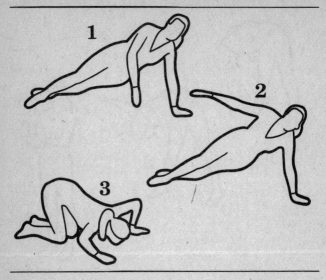

UPPER TORSO/BUST EXERCISE

1. Support yourself on feet and left hand, body extended and facing right, right arm hanging loosely.

2. Swing the right arm straight up as far as possible. Then swing the arm underneath the body. Repeat 10 times with each arm.

3. Kneel on hands and left knee. Bend the right knee to the chest; then extend the right leg straight out in back. Repeat 5 times each leg.

UPPER TORSO/BUST EXERCISE

1. Support yourself on feet and left hand, body extended and facing right, right arm hanging loosely.

2. Circle the right arm in large circles. Repeat 10 times with each arm.

3. Kneel on hands and knees. Bend the elbows and bring the chin to the floor. Straighten the arms and return to starting position. Repeat 10 times.

LATERALS/WAIST EXERCISE

1. Stand, feet slightly apart, knees slightly bent, arms folded across the chest, hands clasping elbows.

2. Lift the left knee to waist height across the body to the right, at the same time bringing the folded arms to waist level at the left side. Return to starting position. Repeat 10 times to each side.

3. Rest 5 counts. With torso erect and head slightly forward, press the knees forward. Place hands behind the thighs and slide the hands down to touch the back of the knees. Stretch and hold. Come to a stand.

LATERALS/WAIST EXERCISE

1. Stand, feet apart, knees slightly bent, both arms overhead.

2. Lift the left knee to waist height across the body to the right, at the same time swinging both arms down to the left and as far back as possible. Return to starting position. Repeat 10 times to each side.

3. Rest 5 counts. Fold arms across the chest, bend knees slightly. Press the pelvis forward. Relax. Repeat 5 times.

DAY FIVE

HIPS/THIGHS/BUTT EXERCISE

1. Stand facing left in a stride position, left leg forward, right leg back, right foot pointing to the side, left foot straight ahead, arms held overhead.

2. Bend the left knee and swing the torso and arms forward and down, the hands touching the left heel. Return to starting position. Repeat 10 times to each side.

3. Stand. Cross both feet so that the toes are turned in toward each other, the heels as far out as possible. Slowly slide the hands to the floor. Hold. Come to a stand. Reverse feet and repeat.

HIPS/THIGHS/BUTT EXERCISE

1. Stand facing left in a stride position, left leg forward, right leg back, right foot pointing to the side, left foot straight ahead, arms held overhead.

2. Bend the left knee and swing torso and arms forward and down, hands touching left foot. As you return to starting position, straighten the left leg and lift the left foot. Repeat 10 times to each side.

3. Lean forward and place hands on the floor. Slide the left leg forward between the hands, right leg straight back. Stretch and hold. Return to starting position. Repeat with the right leg forward, left leg back.

DAY FIVE

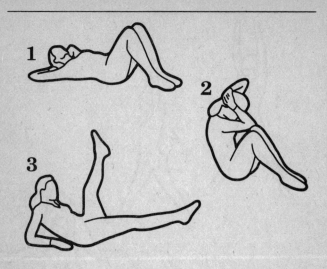

ABDOMINAL EXERCISE

1. Lie on floor, knees bent, feet flat on floor, hands clasped behind head.

2. Curl your body up into a sitting position, at the same time twisting the torso and touching the right elbow to the left knee. Return to starting position. Repeat movement touching the left elbow to the right knee. Alternate 10 times to each side.

3. Lie on the floor, resting on the elbows, legs extended up in open "V" position. Swing the right leg down and to the left as close to the floor as possible. Return to starting position. Repeat 5 times to each side.

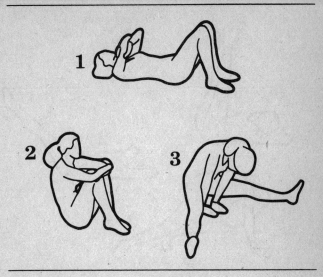

ABDOMINAL EXERCISE

1. Lie on the floor, knees bent, feet slightly off the floor, arms folded at the chest, hands clasping elbows, head up.

2. Sit up, encircling knees with the clasped arms. Lower the body back to the floor, arms across chest, legs extended forward, knees slightly bent, legs slightly off floor. Hold. Repeat 10 times.

3. Sit on the floor, legs wide apart, knees slightly bent, head down, hands on the floor between the legs. Place the weight on the hands, lean forward, and lift the hips off the floor. Repeat 5 times.

DAY FIVE

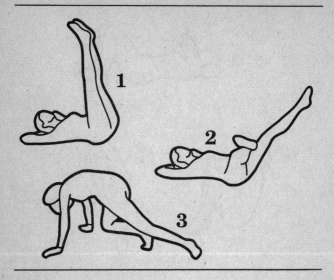

COOL DOWN #1

1. Lie on floor, hands clasped behind the head, legs extended straight up.

2. Open the legs to a wide "V" position, close them; repeat several times while slowly lowering the legs to the floor. Bend the knees to the chest and return to starting position. Repeat 10 times.

3. Stand on hands and feet in a runner's starting position: the right knee bent and slightly forward, the left leg back. Lifting alternate knees to the chest, "run" in place for 20 counts.

COOL DOWN #2

1. Lie on floor, hands clasped behind the head, legs extended straight up.

2. Open the legs to wide "V" position, then alternately cross them left over right, right over left, while slowly lowering the legs to the floor. Bend the knees and return to the starting position. Repeat 10 times.

3. Stand on hands and feet, legs extended straight back in a "push-up" position. Jump, lifting both knees to the chest; then jump back to the starting position. Repeat 10 times.

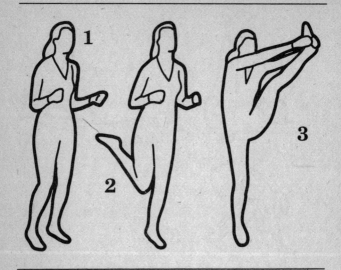

WARM UP #1

1. Stand, feet slightly apart, arms bent at waist height, weight on toes.

2. Run in place, kicking the lower legs as high up in back as possible, for 20 counts on each leg.

3. Stand on right leg. Bend the left knee to the chest, grasp the bottom of the left foot with both hands. Slowly try to straighten the left leg in front of you.

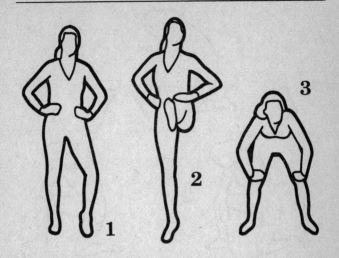

WARM UP #2

1. Stand on right leg with the knee slightly bent; place left leg to the side with the weight on the toes, hands on the hips.

2. Hopping on the right leg, lift the left knee to the chest, then lower the left foot to the floor. Still hopping, kick the left leg straight up. Return to starting position. (Like the cancan!) Repeat 10 times on each leg.

3. Place feet wide apart, knees bent, hands on knees, elbows pointed directly to the side, head down. Turn elbows toward each other, lift head and shoulders, take a deep breath. Hold. Exhale slowly.

NECK/SHOULDERS EXERCISE

1. Kneel on right knee, left foot flat on floor. Hold training weight in right hand, right arm hanging straight down. Place left elbow on the knee to support the back.

2. Circle the right arm from the shoulder 10 times clockwise, then 10 times counterclockwise. Repeat with left arm.

3. Place the weight down. Lower the head. With right hand in a fist, stretch the right arm up overhead as high as possible. Hold for 5 counts. Relax. Repeat with left arm.

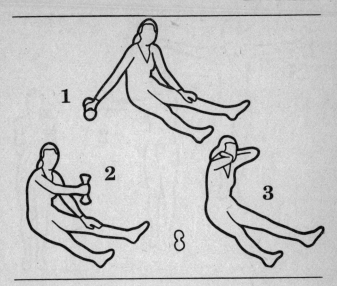

NECK/SHOULDERS EXERCISE

1. Sit on the floor, feet apart, knees slightly bent, head up. Hold the training weight in the right hand on the floor at the right side.

2. Raise the right arm directly out to the side at shoulder height. With a slightly bent elbow, swing the weight forward, stopping directly in front of the chest. Swing back to the side. Repeat 10 times with each arm.

3. With elbows at waist height, place the fingertips of each hand on the shoulder Slowly raise the elbows as high as possible. Hold. Then lower the elbows. Repeat 5 times.

DAY SIX

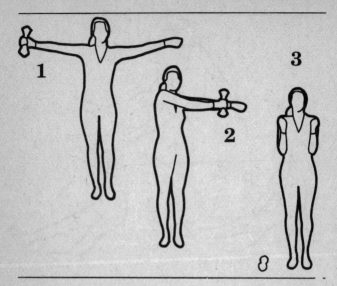

ARMS EXERCISE

1. Stand, feet wide apart, both arms extended to the sides at shoulder height, training weight held in the right hand.

2. Bend the right elbow slightly and swing the right arm across the front of the body to touch the left arm. Swing back to starting position. Repeat 10 times with each arm.

3. Place the training weight down. Press the elbows into the sides, squeeze both hands in a fist. Hold 5 counts. Relax lower arms to the sides and shake them loosely. Repeat 10 times.

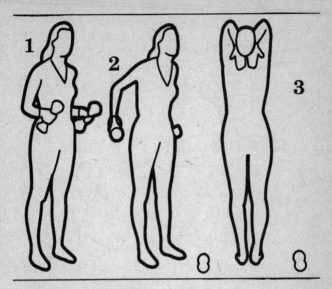

ARMS EXERCISE

1. Stand, feet apart, elbows bent, a training weight in each hand at waist height.

2. Swing the elbows back and up as high as possible. Return to starting position. Repeat 10 times. Do in a fluid motion.

3. Place the training weights down. Put the hands on the shoulders, lift the elbows high and reach down the back as far as possible with the hands. Hold. Relax.

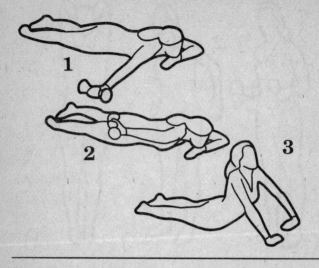

UPPER TORSO/BUST EXERCISE

1. Lie on the floor face down, chin resting on the left hand, right arm directly out to the side at shoulder level, training weight held palm up in the right hand.

2. Raise the right arm up as high as possible. Return to starting position. Repeat 10 times with each arm.

3. Place weights down. Lying face down, place both hands on the floor beneath the chin, fingers turned toward each other. Press the arms to a straight position, lifting the head and torso off the floor.

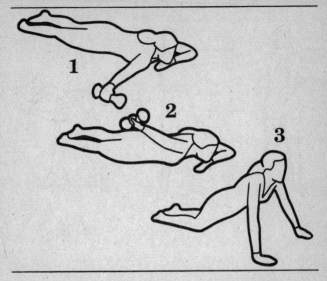

UPPER TORSO/BUST EXERCISE

1. Lie on the floor face down, chin resting on the left hand, right arm directly out to the side at shoulder level, training weight held palm down in the right hand.

2. Raise the right arm up as high as possible. Return to starting position. Repeat 10 times with each arm.

3. Place the weight down. Still lying on the floor, place both hands on the floor at shoulder width, fingers straight ahead. Press the arms to a straight position, lifting the head and torso off the floor.

DAY SIX

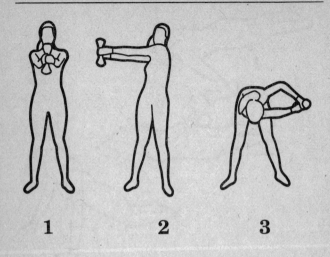

1 **2** **3**

LATERALS/WAIST EXERCISE

1. Stand, feet apart, body erect, training weight held in both hands, arms extended directly in front of the chest.

2. Swing the arms to the right as far as possible, then swing back to the left as far as possible. (Keep the feet stationary.) Repeat 10 times.

3. Bend forward at the waist. Swing the training weight directly to the left as far as possible, then swing back to the right as far as possible. Repeat 10 times.

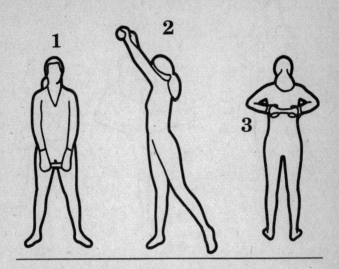

LATERALS/WAIST EXERCISE

1. Stand, feet wide apart, body erect, training weight held in both hands, arms hanging loosely forward.

2. Pivot on the left foot and swing the weight to the right, extending it over the right shoulder as high as possible. Swing back to starting position and repeat movement to the left. Alternate 10 times to each side.

3. Hold the training weight behind the back, arms relaxed. Bend the elbows and lift the training weight up the back as high as possible. Lower the weight. Repeat 10 times.

DAY SIX

HIPS/THIGHS/BUTT EXERCISE

1. Stand on left leg, hands on hips, right leg extended to the side, training weight on right ankle.

2. Raise the right leg directly to the right side as high as possible. Lower the leg. Repeat 10 times with each leg.

3. Remove the weight. Stand on the left leg. Lift the right knee above the waist, encircling it with both hands; then extend the right leg back at the same time thrusting both arms up overhead. Repeat 10 times with each leg.

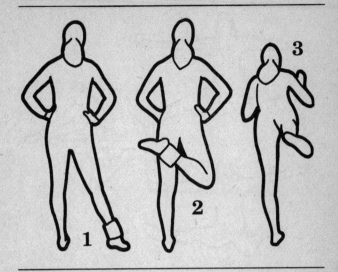

HIPS/THIGHS/BUTT EXERCISE

1. Stand on left leg, hands on hips, right leg extended to the side, training weight on right ankle.

2. Bending at the knee, lift the right lower leg up and across the back of the left leg as high as possible. Lower leg. Repeat 10 times with each leg.

3. Remove the training weight. Place hands against a wall. Stand on left leg approximately 12" from the wall, right leg to the side. Raise right leg back as high as possible. Lower the leg. Repeat 10 times with each leg.

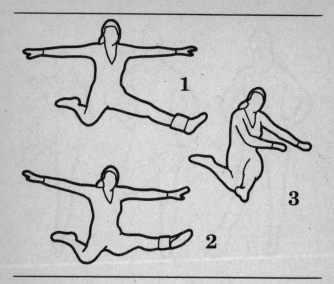

ABDOMINAL EXERCISE

1. Sit in a straddle position, right leg bent back, left leg extended to the side, arms extended directly to the sides at shoulder height, training weight on the left ankle.

2. Raise the left leg as high as possible. Lower leg. Repeat 10 times with each leg.

3. Remove training weight. Return to straddle position. Lift left leg off the floor; swing it to the right, at the same time swinging both arms to the left. Swing leg back to the left, arms back to the right. Repeat 5 times with each leg.

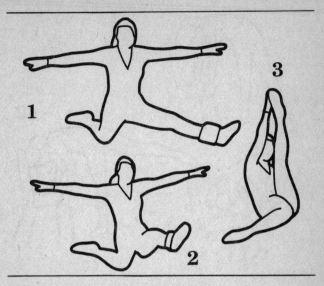

ABDOMINAL EXERCISE

1. Sit in a straddle position, right leg bent back, left leg extended to the side, arms extended directly to the sides at shoulder height.

2. Raise the left leg and move it in circles for 10 revolutions. Repeat with the right leg.

3. Remove the training weight. Return to straddle position. Lean on left forearm and elbow, lift right arm up. Raise the left leg and touch the right hand to the left foot. Lower leg. Repeat 5 times with each leg.

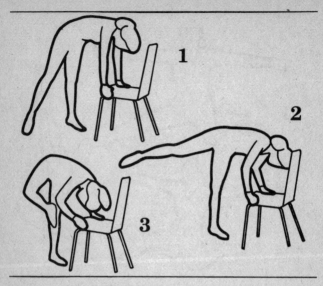

COOL DOWN #1

1. Stand on left leg, hands on seat of chair, arms straight, right leg to the side, torso over floor. (No weights used.)

2. Lift the right leg up and back, then swing it out to the side at shoulder height, pivoting on the left toe. Swing the leg back. Lower leg to starting position. Repeat 10 times on each leg.

3. Stand, hands on seat of chair, arms straight, weight on left leg. Place sole of the right foot on the inside of the left knee, the right knee pointing to side. Bend elbows and bring head down to chair. Reverse position of legs and repeat.

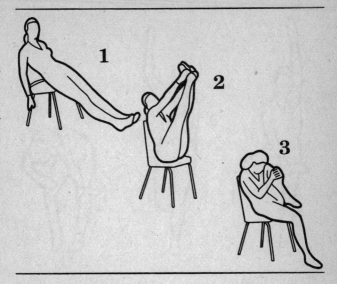

COOL DOWN #2

1. Sit on a chair, hips at edge of chair, hands holding chair, heels on floor. (No weights used.)

2. Bend the knees to the chest, grasp the soles of the feet with both hands. Slowly try to straighten the legs as far as you can. (Don't force the stretch.) Hold. Repeat. (Do this only when the muscles are warmed up.)

3. Sit on chair, feet on floor. Pull the left knee to the chest with the hands. Bend the head forward and try to touch the nose to the knee. Hold. Repeat with the right leg.

WARM UP #1

1. Stand on right leg, left knee bent. Grasp left ankle with left hand. Extend right arm overhead. Hop on right leg 5 counts.

2. Still hopping, rotate left knee; lift lower leg in back. Grasp left ankle with right hand and extend left arm overhead. Hop for 5 counts. Repeat for total of 20 counts on each leg.

3. Lean forward, feet together, hands on knees, fingers inward. Bend the left knee, lift left heel high, while pressing on the right leg with the right hand. Return. Alternate 10 times with each leg.

WARM UP #2

1. Stand, arms at sides. Hop continuously on right foot. At the same time, kick left leg straight forward as high as possible and swing arms forward toward left foot; lower arms and left leg.

2. While still hopping on right foot, kick left leg straight out to left side and extend both arms out to the sides; lower arms and leg. Repeat 5 times on each leg.

3. Lean forward, feet together, head down, knees slightly bent, hands on knees, fingers turned inward. Turn heels out to the side as far as possible. Return to starting position. Repeat 10 times.

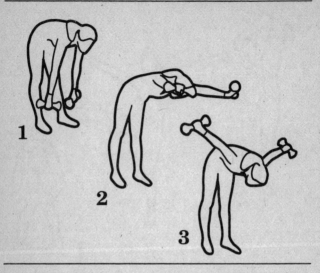

NECK/SHOULDERS EXERCISE

1. Stand, feet apart, torso bent forward at the waist, back flat, head relaxed, a training weight held in each hand, arms hanging loosely.

2. Swing the training weights forward to head height, then lower weights to starting position. Repeat 10 times.

3. Continue to hold training weights. With the head down, the back rounded and the arms hanging loosely, swing both weights straight out to the sides as high as possible. Lower to starting position. Repeat 10 times.

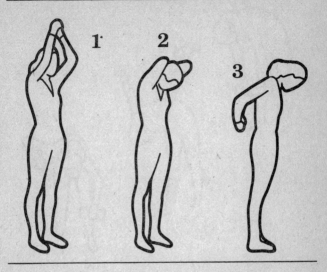

NECK/SHOULDERS EXERCISE

1.   Stand, feet apart, hands clasped, arms up, elbows bent at eye level.

2.   Place the hands on the back of the neck and lower the head. Hold. Return to starting position. Repeat 10 times.

3.   Place the arms behind the back, clasp the wrists, and raise the arms as high as possible. Lower arms, turn the shoulders back and stretch.

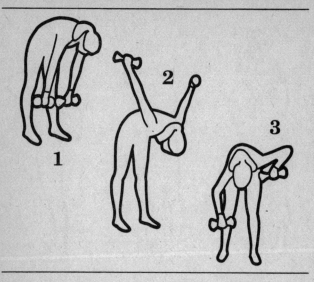

NECK/SHOULDERS EXERCISE

1. Stand, feet apart, torso bent forward at waist, back rounded, head down, a training weight held in each hand, arms hanging loosely, palms facing backward.

2. Swing the arms back, then up and out to the sides, keeping the palms turned toward the ceiling. Lower arms. Repeat 10 times.

3. Continue to hold weights. With the head down, the back rounded and the arms hanging loosely, bend the left elbow and pull the weight to chest height. Lower weight. Repeat with the right arm. Alternate with each arm 10 times.

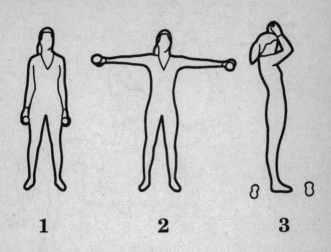

1 **2** **3**

ARMS EXERCISE

1. Stand, feet apart, body erect, a training weight held in each hand, arms at sides.

2. Raise arms directly to sides at shoulder height, bend arms and touch weights to shoulders, extend arms overhead, return weights to shoulders, extend arms directly to the sides at shoulder height, lower arms to starting position. Repeat 10 times.

3. Place weights down. Elbows bent, clasp hands at eye level. Touch elbows together and raise arms until elbows are at eye level. Stretch. Lower arms. Repeat 5 times.

DAY SEVEN

ARMS EXERCISE

1. Support weight on hands and toes in push-up position, fingers facing forward.

2. Lower both knees to the floor, then raise the hips as high as possible. Repeat 10 times with fingers forward, 10 times with fingers back.

3. Kneel on hands and knees. Shift weight to toes and fingertips, and lift the knees up off the floor. Hold. Relax.

ARMS EXERCISE

1. Stand, feet wide apart, a training weight held in each hand, arms at sides.

2. Swing the arms directly to the sides and up overhead, crossing the wrists. Lower to starting position. Repeat 10 times.

3. Hold the training weights at the sides, palms forward. Press the elbows into the sides, bend the elbows, and raise the weights to the shoulders. Slowly lower weights to starting position. Repeat 10 times.

DAY SEVEN

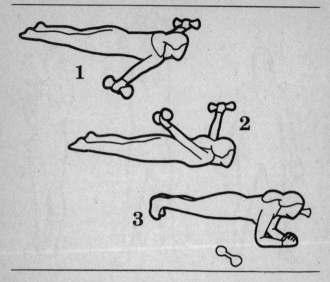

UPPER TORSO/BUST EXERCISE

1. Lie on the floor face down, chin resting on the floor, both arms directly to the sides at shoulder level, a training weight held palms down in each hand.

2. Raise both arms straight up as high as possible. Lower arms to floor. Repeat 10 times.

3. Place the weights down; clasp the hands; rest the body weight on the elbows, forearms, and toes. Lift the body off the floor. Lower body. Repeat 5 times.

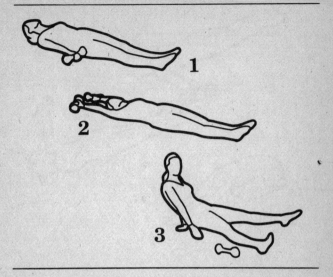

UPPER TORSO/BUST EXERCISE

1. Lie flat on back, arms at sides. Hold a training weight in each hand, palms up.

2. Swing the arms along the floor to a position behind the head, keeping the weights slightly off the floor throughout. Swing weights back to sides. Repeat 10 times.

3. Place the training weights down. Come to a sitting position, feet wide apart. Support body weight on the heels and the left hand and lift the hips off the floor. Move the right arm in large circles 10 times. Repeat with the left arm.

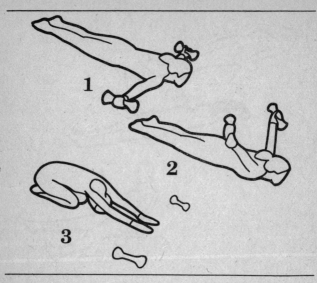

UPPER TORSO/BUST EXERCISE

1. Lie on the floor face down, chin resting on the floor, both arms directly to the sides at shoulder level, a training weight held palms up in each hand.

2. Raise both arms straight up as high as possible. Lower arms to the floor. Repeat 10 times.

3. Kneel, hips on heels, hands on floor, torso bent slightly forward, head down. Touch the chest to the thighs, extend the arms forward, and press the head between the arms. Stretch. Hold. Relax.

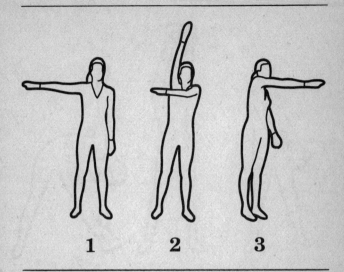

1   **2**   **3**

LATERALS/WAIST EXERCISE

1. Stand, feet wide apart, left arm at side, right arm extended directly to the side at shoulder height.

2. Raise the right arm straight up overhead, at the same time moving the left arm across the chest. Return to starting position. Repeat 10 times; reverse arm positions and repeat 10 more times.

3. Stand, arms at sides. Extend the right arm forward at shoulder height, twisting the arms so that the palm is turned toward the ceiling. Hold. Return to starting position. Repeat 5 times with each arm.

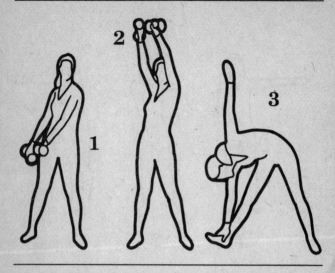

LATERALS/WAIST EXERCISE

1. Stand, feet apart, toes forward, head and torso slightly to the right, arms at right side, a training weight in each hand.

2. Swing both weights along the right side to the overhead position. Repeat 10 times to each side.

3. Place weights down. Stand, feet wide apart. Turn right foot to side and grasp right ankle with right hand. Extend left arm straight up and lift right toe off the floor as high as possible. Repeat 5 times to each side.

LATERALS/WAIST EXERCISE

1. Stand, hands on the hips, feet wide apart, knees straight.

2. Bend the torso forward and to the right, then swing it low to the left; lift the torso up and back to the left, then bend to the right. The movement should be fluid and circular. Repeat 5 times in each direction.

3. From starting position, lean forward, flatten the back, and lift the head. "Bounce" the torso toward the floor 5 times.

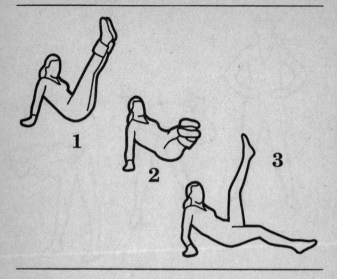

HIPS/THIGHS/BUTT EXERCISE

1. Lie on the floor, resting on elbows, legs extended straight up, training weights on both ankles.

2. Lower both legs to the floor on the right. Return to starting position. Repeat 10 times to each side.

3. Remove training weights. Return to starting position. Move the right leg in a large circle extending all the way to the floor. Repeat 5 times with each leg.

HIPS/THIGHS/BUTT EXERCISE

1. Stand with the left foot forward, right leg to the side, right toe out, both arms overhead and to the right side.

2. Bend the left knee and cross the right leg behind the left and over to the left side, at the same time swinging the arms down and stretching the right arm to the left side. Repeat 10 times to each side.

3. Come to a stride position, right leg forward, left leg back, left toe turned to side, arms extended to sides, right knee bent, torso bent over right knee. Straighten right leg. Bend. Repeat 5 times to each side.

HIPS/THIGHS/BUTT EXERCISE

1. Lie on the back, arms extended at sides, right leg extended forward on the floor, left leg extended directly up, training weights on both ankles.

2. Keeping the legs straight, lower the left leg directly to the right side, touching the left foot to the right hand. Return to starting position. Repeat 10 times with each leg. Remove weights.

3. Sit, right leg extended forward, left knee bent, left foot and right hand flat on the floor. Lift hips high off the floor and extend the left arm behind the head. Stretch. Relax. Repeat to the right side.

ABDOMINAL EXERCISE

1. Lie on the floor, resting on elbows, knees bent, feet flat on the floor, a training weight on each ankle.

2. Bend the knees to the chest, slowly extend the legs out at a 45-degree angle. Bend knees to chest. Repeat 10 times.

3. Remove training weights. Lie on back, arms at sides, legs extended straight forward. Raise the left leg straight up. Lower leg to floor. Repeat with the right leg. Alternate with each leg 10 times.

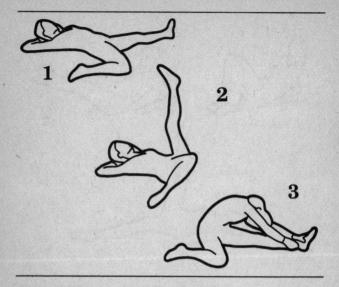

ABDOMINAL EXERCISE

1. Lie on floor in a straddle position, hands clasped behind head, right leg bent back, left leg extended forward and slightly to the side.

2. Raise the left leg straight up. Lower leg to the floor. Repeat 10 times with each leg.

3. Sit in a straddle position, right leg bent back, left leg extended straight forward. Bend torso forward, grasp the left ankle with both hands Stretch. Relax. Repeat with the right leg.

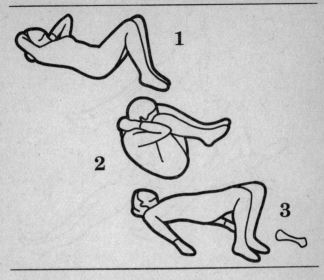

ABDOMINAL EXERCISE

1. Lie on back, knees bent, feet flat on the floor, training weight held in both hands behind the neck.

2. Curl body up into a sitting position and try to bring the head to the knees. Lower body to floor. Repeat 10 times.

3. Place the training weight down. Lie on back, knees bent, feet flat on the floor, arms at sides. Lift hips off the floor. Arch back. Hold. Return hips to floor. Repeat.

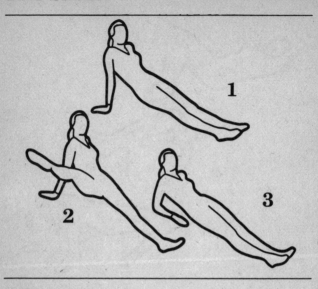

COOL DOWN #1

1. With back towards floor, support yourself on heels and hands, feet together, arms and legs straight, head up, body off floor.

2. Swing the right leg directly to the side as far as possible. Return to starting position. Repeat 5 times with each leg.

3. Lower the hips to the floor, rest on elbows. Lift hips off the floor, extend body straight from shoulders to toes. Lower hips to floor. Repeat 5 times.